DISCLAIMER

This course contains the opinions and ideas of its author. It is intended to provide helpful and informative material on the subjects addressed in the course. It is sold with the understanding that the author is not engaged in rendering medical, health or any other kind of professional services in this course. The listener should consult his or her medical, health or other competent professional before adopting any of the suggestions in this course or drawing inferences from it. The author specifically disclaim all responsibility for any liability, loss or risk, personal or otherwise, which is incurred as a consequence, directly or indirectly of the use and application of any of the contents of this course.

By starting this course
you have already set the
intention to connect with
the angelic realm.

Living life with the angels
is about connecting to
the angelic realm and
enhancing your life.

CONTENTS

Disclaimer — 1

Objectives Of This Course — 6

How To Get The Most From This Course — 7

Why you should open up to the angels — 9

Who are the 15 main archangels — 11

Preparing your house — 19

Preparing your body — 22

Preparing your mind — 25

How you can call upon the angels directly — 28

Signs you may receive from the angels — 32

Hearing the angels — 35

Seeing the angels — 38

How to feel the angels — 42

Using angel cards — 44

Angel crystals — 49

Going with the flow in life — 54

Grounding — 56

OBJECTIVES OF THIS COURSE

1. How to get the most from this course
2. Why you should open up to the angels
3. Who are the 12 main archangels
4. Preparing your house
5. Preparing your body
6. Preparing your mind
7. How you can call upon the angels directly
8. Signs you may receive from the angels
9. Hearing the angels
10. Seeing the angels
11. How to feel the angels
12. Using angel cards
13. Angel crystals
14. Going with the flow in life
15. Grounding

HOW TO GET THE MOST FROM THIS COURSE

You may decide to do an objective of the course each week. This will mean you do not need to rush each section and will allow you to take in the information.

Each course objective contains only the most important bits of knowledge so that you can learn quickly and efficiently without being overwhelmed.

Each chapter contains a 'chapter activity' allowing you the opportunity to practice what you have been taught. Some people learn mostly by doing rather than just reading. If you are one of those types of learners, the chapter activity will be most valuable and help you to gain the most from this course.

It is not imperative that you do all of the chapter activities, but try to do so if you feel guided to.

You can pick and choose the chapters that call out to you. Just as with the chapter activities, you do not have to read and follow every single chapter.

If you feel guided then read the chapter and then if you feel guided to do so, do the chapter activity.

Between the course chapters there may be a popular quote. These can be used to give you a chance to reflect or the quotes can also

be used as something to meditate on. It is up to you how you util-
ise these quotes.

If you feel stuck on a particular course objective/ chapter, just
move on to the next one. You can always go back at a later date if
you want to.

The course is not set out in any particular chronological order,
so when looking at the objectives of this course, if one pulls out
strongly to you, then go to that one first.

WHY YOU SHOULD OPEN UP TO THE ANGELS

By opening up to the angels you're allowing yourself to be supported by the universe. You're opening up to a world of magic and a faith that everything will be ok in the end.

Anyone can open up and communicate with the angels, you don't need to be an expert psychic or even *gifted*, and you don't have to belong to any or particular religion.

All you need is an open mind and an open heart. Humans have been connecting with the angels for centuries.

Everyone will have a unique relationship with the angels, but the angels have helped and continue to give people strength and hope during hard and emotional times.

The angels are also happy to help you with trivial issues such as finding the perfect parking space, to helping you find lost items. There is no judgement from the angels, they just want you to be happy.

Feel happier than ever when you have the angels around you, as you feel safe and content, and know you are protected from negative energy.

Angels know we have free will, so they can only help and assist us if we call upon them.

As our spiritual protectors, the angels are important to call upon if you attempt to contact the spiritual realm such as when practicing mediumship or even practicing magic and spells. By calling upon the angels, they can make sure you are safe and keep negative beings and energy away.

Chapter Activity: Take a deep breath, and use this affirmation before you go to sleep and when you wake up - "I am ready to receive from the angels and communicate to the angels with ease."

An affirmation is a positive statement about you/ your life/ situation to the universe. The above affirmation will put it out to the universe that you are ready to communicate with the angels.

WHO ARE THE 15 MAIN ARCHANGELS

The archangels are extra powerful angels that oversee the angels. We can call upon the archangels just like we do for the angels.

The archangels are able to be in many places at the same time, so an important lesson about working with the archangels is that you are never taking them away from helping someone in a life threatening situation.

Archangel Ariel:

Archangel Ariel is the beautiful archangel that can be called upon to help us in times when we may need more money or if there are any housing issues, but she is also great to call upon for any environmental issues that you may be dealing with. For example you can call upon Ariel to help with any environmental problems that are happening near you home such as fracking, or coastal erosion.

If you have a pet that is sick you can call upon Ariel to help with healing or to bring more loving energy to your pet. Also try calling upon Ariel to help other animals you see in the world who are being mistreated by human beings.

Archangel Azrael:

Archangel Azrael helps with souls that have passed over from Earth on to heaven. If someone has recently passed away then call upon archangel Azrael to help them on to heaven. If you are grieving over a death and departed loved one then Azrael can be called upon to help you heal and to move on from the grief.

He is sometimes known as the angel of death to some cultures but do not worry as archangel Azrael is there to help souls that are already departed loved ones and is there to help show them the light.

Archangel Chamuel:

Archangel Chamuel is the archangel to call upon when praying for world peace. He can help ease any anxious emotions you may have and can be called upon to help find any lost objects. For example if you have recently lost a piece of jewellery, call upon Chamuel to help you relocate it.

Archangel Chamuel is one of the archangels that is mentioned in the Kabbalah, but as with all angels, they are non denominational which means anyone from any religion, creed or colour can call upon them.

Archangel Gabriel:

Archangel Gabriel is perhaps most famous for his role in the nativity story. His name means messenger of God. Call upon Gabriel to help you if you have writers block or if you're a teacher.

You can also call upon Gabriel if you ever need help involving children, including conception or if you are considering adoption or fostering.

Archangel Haniel:

Archangel Haniel is another of the archangels that is mentioned in the Kabbalah. She is the perfect archangel to call upon to help with a woman's monthly cycle, but can also be called upon to help increase your clairvoyance abilities.

Archangel Haniel is the perfect archangel to call upon for any budding spiritualists and mediums as she can help give you clearer visions and a stronger connection.

Archangel Jeremiel:

Archangel Jeremiel can be called upon to help us with forgiveness. Sometimes the best healing we can do in a situation is forgiveness. While it may seem a hard task to do, by calling on Jeremiel, he can help give you the strength to find forgiveness for others and yourself as well as helping to keep your emotions calm and peaceful.

Archangel Jophiel:

Archangel Jophiel is the angel of beauty. She can help neutralise any negative energy and will help beautify any spaces like your home or office as well as your thoughts. She is the ideal archangel to call upon if you're an artist or in a creative industry.

Archangel Metatron:

Archangel Metatron is the archangel that can help you to heal any childhood issues or abandonment issues. If you have any crystal or indigo children then Metatron is the perfect archangel to call upon.

Archangel Michael:

Archangel Michael is one of the most famous archangels. He is a protector and will clear away any negative energy or entities. Call upon him to remove any fear from your life. Archangel Michael is mentioned in many religious texts including Christianity, Islam and Jewish.

Archangel Raguel:

Archangel Raguel will bring peace to your relationships. If you have recently had a fall out with a friend or family member, call upon Raguel to heal the relationship and to bring back the harmony and peace. Raguel will make any communications you have to be harmonious, peaceful and filled with love and clear understandings.

Archangel Raphael:

Archangel Raphael is the healing angel. His natural ability to help heal and to assist others in healing is powerful. If you're ill or about to go in to surgery then call upon archangel Raphael to bring healing, the knowledge needed and strength.

Archangel Raziel:

Archangel Raziel is the archangel to call upon if you're undergoing a past life regression. This is when you view a life you have lived previously, usually via guided hypnosis. You can also call upon Raziel if you want some help with any dream interpretations, or if you facing any psychic blocks that may be preventing you from receiving clear communication from the spirit world. If you are interested in mediumship, call upon him.

Archangel Sandalphon:

Archangel Sandalphon is the one to call upon if you're a musician. He can help you create and play music which will inspire and heal all those who listen to it. If you have or know someone with a naturally aggressive personality then you can call upon archangel Sandalphon to remove any aggressive energy and bring a calming peaceful energy to yourself and the person in question.

Archangel Uriel:

Archangel Uriel is the archangel of wisdom and intellect. Ask him to help if you're studying for an exam or in need of some inspirational ideas. He is also great at helping you feel motivated to revise.

Uriel is regarded as one of the 4 main archangels, the others being Michael, Raphael and Gabriel.

Archangel Zadkiel:

Archangel Zadkiel is the archangel that can help with any mental difficulties that you may be facing including stress or memory issues. He is another useful archangel to call upon before an exam. Archangel Zadkiel is also one of the archangels that is mentioned in the Kabbalah.

So there we have 15 of the most popular archangels. Even if you're new to angels you may have heard of Archangel Michael. He is one of the most powerful archangels and is a great protector.

You can call upon archangel Michael to cleanse your home and your aura from negative energy.

Working with individual archangels can be a rewarding relationship once you get to sense that each has a unique feeling and energy to them.

During your spiritual journey you may come across other archangels that aren't included in this list.

Chapter Activity: This chapter activity involves a very simple meditation. It will include the four archangels, Michael, Raphael, Uriel and Chamuel. So find a quiet place where you will not be disturbed, though if you find it soothing and you are guided to do so, have some peaceful music playing in the background but avoid any music with lyrics.

While you are getting into a meditative state, I want you to call upon all four of the archangels. (You can do this in your head if you prefer).

Calling upon archangel Michael I want you to imagine a royal purple light covering your entire body, and to ask archangel Michael to cleanse you from negative energy, low vibrational beings and to cut any cords of anger and hatred.

Have a few moments of deep breathing to let archangel Michael carry out his healing.

Calling upon archangel Raphael I want you to now imagine a vivid green light covering your entire body, and ask archangel Raphael to heal your body of any physical ailments and to heal any emotional scars.

Have a few moments of deep breathing so that archangel Raphael can carry out his healing.

Calling upon archangel Uriel I want you to imagine a red/orangey light covering your body, and to ask archangel Uriel to remove any miscommunication from your relationships and to heal any resentment that you may have to others.

Have a few moments of deep breathing so that archangel Uriel can carry out this healing.

Call upon archangel Chamuel and imagine a beautiful pale pink light covering your body. I want you to then ask archangel Chamuel to remove any anxious feelings and emotions that you may have, and to bring peace and calm to your own life and to Earth.

Have a few moments of deep breathing so that archangel Chamuel can do his healing.

Once you feel ready to come out of the meditation, remember to thank the archangels for their healing today.

This meditation can be amended to fit any of your favourite archangels, so feel free to try working with different archangels each week.

"There are no accidents … there is only some
purpose that we haven't yet understood."

- Deepak Chopra

PREPARING YOUR HOUSE

Preparing your house is not absolutely necessary but can help you to focus your mind and set the intention of connecting with the angels.

By preparing your house and following the guidance in this chapter you will help create the perfect conditions for the angels to connect to you and to witness their signs.

Tip 1: Cleaning

As the saying goes, 'a clear house, a clear mind'. Removing clutter from your room or house can help remove negative blocked energy, As in the practice of Feng shui, by removing unwanted rubbish and items you are allowing the universal life force to flow naturally through your home.

When cleaning your house, the angels would always prefer us to use eco friendly products where we possibly can. Harsh and toxic chemicals can block the angels signs but by being more considerate of the Earth you may find that you'll gain the support of the fairy realm.

Tip 2: Fresh air

Open your windows, let the fresh air circulate around your house. This will help clear stale and stagnant energy throughout your house.

Not only will you feel the difference energetically, you will also notice the difference when you breath.

Tip 3: Smudging

Smudging is the burning of herbs, the most popular used is white sage. The smoke caused from burning sage removes negative energy and beings. It is commonly used by people who move in to a new home to rid the space of the previous tenants energy.

Some people like to use smudge sticks when going to clear a haunted house. If you find smudge sticks hard to get or quite expensive, then you can use the smoke from burning incense.

Chapter Activity: Go round your entire house burning a smudge stick and ask archangel Michael to clear negative energy and low vibrational beings from your house. See if you notice a difference in the energy of your house after doing this activity.

PREPARING YOUR BODY

While connecting with the angels is a very spiritual thing to do and involves the mind and visualising, it is also important to maintain that your body is healthy and well. Your human physical body is the vessel that your soul travels in when you are here on Earth. It's important to respect your body and to look after it.

When your body isn't filled with harmful toxins and unhealthy foods you will begin to feel your spiritual connection to the angels and the spirit realm is stronger.

Tip 1: Sea salt bath

Cleanse your body with a sea salt bath. Sea salt baths are used to ease the muscles and help the body to detox. In a spiritual view, they are great to both relax your mind and purify your soul. Salt is often used in spell work to cleanse and protect a space.

Once you have found some bath salts that you like, follow the instructions on the packet. Take some deep breaths while you're in the sea salt bath and visualise the bath water as white light cleansing over your body.

Tip 2: Exercise

Exercise is one of the greatest ways to prepare the body for connecting with the angels. Not only are you maintaining a healthy body that your soul resides in, but also you'll be releasing feel good endorphins which help to raise your spiritual vibration.

You may find in this course and other spiritual books you have read or if you've tried meditating the importance of deep breathing and receiving oxygen in to the body. Exercise will help you do just that!

Tips 3: Eating healthy

Following a healthy and balanced diet will help keep your body healthy. Remember to eat lots of fresh fruit and vegetables in to your diet and try to buy organic when possible.

Buy eating a healthy diet you are reducing the amount of harmful substances entering your body that can reduce your psychic abilities.

Chapter Activity: Go for a walk or run. Try to choose a walk or run that is in nature. A local park or nature reserve would be perfect. Just go with your thoughts and ask the angels any questions that you have. See what responses you get in the form of thoughts, feelings or even scents and sounds.

PREPARING YOUR MIND

Being in the right frame of mind will help you to connect with the angels but more importantly it will help you be more receptive and notice the signs that the angels are sending your way.

Raising your spiritual vibration is an important stage when you are wanting to communicate with the angels. Being in a higher spiritual vibration means that you are getting on their level. High vibrational is feelings of joy, happiness, glee, while low vibrational energy which can attract less appealing spirits are feelings of hatred, anger, worry and fear!

Tip 1: Meditation

Meditation is a skill to practice that will help you quieten your mind. With a quieter mind, you are more likely to *hear* the messages you are receiving from the angels. It will also help you to decipher which are your own thoughts and which are thoughts from the angels giving you guidance and help.

Tip 2: Forgiving yourself and others

Forgiving yourself is important in helping you release tension and anxiety. While this may not be an overnight success in doing, it's important that you start to set an intention that you forgive yourself. No one is perfect and some lessons in life are to make mistakes. It's often how we can learn and grow.

Include it in your meditation, use affirmations such as 'I forgive myself', experiment with the use of such affirmations if you struggle to forgive yourself for something that may make you be feeling guilty for what you have done in the past.

If you have done something that you deem bad and you feel guilty of, try to remember or even make a list of all the good deeds that you have done.

Tip 3: Being thankful

Similar to what was mentioned in the previous tip, it will also raise your vibration and bring you out of a *slump.* Try to note everything that you do have thankful to be for in your life.

Even as simple as having a place to sleep at night is something that not everyone has the privilege of. Take a moment and look around, you will soon realise there is plenty to be thankful for.

Chapter Activity: This chapter activity will help you to feel relaxed, but also help you in learning to quieten your mind. There is nothing to visualise, it is simply sitting still and quietly in the now.

So find yourself a quiet space where you can sit in peace. Pick a time where you know the chance of you being distracted is low. Don't play any music or sounds. Set a timer for 10 minutes and begin. If you find yourself getting distracted by a thought, that's fine, just acknowledge it and save it for later.

You may find this activity useful to practice on a lunch break at work, maybe if you have access to a car it creates a rather quiet and undisturbed space.

Over time you will find this activity easier and easier, but it will also benefit you in meditation. It will allow you to slow your thoughts down and gradually learn which thoughts are your own and which are messages coming from the spiritual realms and the angels.

HOW YOU CAN CALL UPON THE ANGELS DIRECTLY

Speaking out loud

If you're not the shy type, you can ask for the angels help out loud as though you're talking to a friend. Speaking out loud is not any better or any worse than the other methods of calling upon the angels, however it is all down to personal preference. Some people prefer to speak out loud as it can feel more *real* for them to do. Try it and experiment. If you are not keen on speaking out loud to the angels, try one of the other methods in this chapter.

Thinking

This is a popular way that people like to call upon the angels as it allows you to ask the angels for help in private and without judgement from those around you that are less open to spirituality. Just think to yourself what you would like to ask the angels. It can be as simple as 'angels please help today be filled with positive energy and may everyone I come in to contact with be happy and joyful'.

Just as with any of the other methods of calling upon the angels, you can call upon the angels at any time. When you just wake up, to when you are about to fall asleep, even in your dreams!

Prayer and affirmations

This can be done using either of the two previous methods. Saying out loud or thinking, using prayer and affirmations is a great direct way to call upon the angels and the universe. Affirmations are useful if you're trying to view life in a more positive way. Using affirmations such as 'today will be a good day' or 'the angels support me in my life mission' are good examples.

Using prayers are good if you're unsure what to say to the angels or if you're feeling worried of saying the wrong thing (you can't by the way, the angels will never judge you). Pre written prayers such as from our archangel prayer book, are useful to quickly find an appropriate prayer for what you are needing in that very moment.

Visualisation

Visualising the angels around you, will summon there energy. You can visualise the angels using coloured light. Imagine a glowing white light. The archangels each have an associated colour to them so if you want to summon archangel Michael imagine the light as a purple/blue colour.

Visualising coloured lights can be used in many effective ways to ask for the protection of the angels. If you want to protect your house or car imagine the angels white light coating your entire house and car. You can even do this visualisation of the entire globe.

Imagining a green light on any parts of your body that needs healing will help summon archangel Raphael (the healing archangel) to assist in healing that part of your body you are focusing on.

Singing

Singing is similar to speaking out loud, but is a great confidence builder. Singing is also a joyful activity which will in turn raise your spiritual vibration. You can sing hymns or even lyrics to your favourite songs. The important thing here is your intention that you are singing to connect to the angels.

Writing

Write to the angels like you're writing a letter to a close friend. If you are someone who is unsure how to put certain thoughts in to speech, then you may find writing to the angels easier and your preferred method. Try to select a special note pad that you use for communications to the angels so it becomes a piece of sacred stationary.

Remember to use a mix of the above methods to get the most from your communications with the angels.

Chapter Activity: In this chapter activity, I want you to grab a pen and paper, you are going to write 3 affirmations that you will then repeat throughout the day. Try it for a week and see if you notice a difference in your outlook on life. Getting in to the habit of using positive affirmations can take time, but the benefits are real and can be life changing for some people. Some examples could be:

"The angels always support and guide me to where I need to go."

"The angels keep my car safe when I'm driving on the roads."

"I'm always protected by archangel Michael and his army of angels."

SIGNS YOU MAY RECEIVE FROM THE ANGELS

Feelings

Feelings are probably going to be the most common way that the angels may respond to us. If you are used to listening to your intuition you may be more familiar at noticing these feelings and how to understand these feelings more clearly.

Just think of when you meet someone for the first time. You tend to ask yourself both consciously and subconsciously whether they are trustworthy. Try to recall a situation where your feelings give you clear guidance as to whether the person is someone you should trust or should avoid.

When we ask the angels a question, try to notice a shift in your feelings, have your feelings suddenly filled with butterflies in the stomach or have you started to feel hopeful and full of glee.

Feelings are a great way to connect to the angels and it can take some practice. Knowing your inner feelings and being able to differentiate them clearly in your mind is also useful for divination such as reading angel cards.

Smell of roses

If you suddenly start to smell the scent of roses, this could be a sign that the angels are near to you. I often find I get this during meditation where there is no other possible source that the rose scent is coming from. Sometimes the angels and spirits can also use other scents to get our attention. You may suddenly start to smell a loved ones aftershave that they used to wear, or even smell something bad if you are being warned about someone.

Coins/ Feathers

From time to time the angels will like to leave us little feathers to show us that they are nearby. They tend to be small white feathers, and you will often find them in places where you would be unlikely to find them.

Ideas

When we ask for help from the angels, their help may come in the form of ideas. For example, if we asked the angels to help with a business, you may start to get ideas on how to make your business more efficient or what product you should sell next.

Orbs of light

From time to time you may see spiritual beings or the angels as orbs of light flying around in the corner of your eye line. Usually lasting a fleeting second or two, try to recognise the colour of the orb. It may be a particular archangel that is present. They tend to appear when you're coming out of a meditative state and not trying to force the appearance of a light orb.

Sounds

Some people may hear the angels in an audible voice or even having a particular song play on the radio.

Hearing the angels is covered in more detail in the next chapter.

Clouds

Clouds have been used for hundreds of years as a form of divination. The angels will sometimes give us signs in the form of clouds. When looking up at the sky, you may notice a cloud looks like a particular country, or object that may relate to a question that you have the asked the angels about.

Chapter Activity: For this chapter activity, I want you to find a quiet place where you won't be disturbed. Grab a notepad and pen and start to take deep breaths. Ask the angels a question that you have for them. Try and quiet your mind and then make a note of any ideas or feelings that you start to receive.

These ideas in your head and feelings in your body are signs from the angels. By writing them down, you won't have the problem of forgetting and you can take a look at your notes at a later date.

HEARING THE ANGELS

Hearing the angels is an affirming way of knowing they are with you. You may not hear the angels as a voice speaking directly to you, it may be that you pick up on a nearby conversation that answers the question you have been asking to the angels, or it may even be a particular song suddenly playing when you change a radio station.

The angels like to surprise by communicating in ways that we may not necessarily expect.

Songs

Imagine the situation, you're driving to work and you keep asking the angels in your head to make this day a great day. Next song on the radio is 'It's a beautiful day' by Michael Bublé. Now this may seem a coincidence to some people, or some may not even pick up on this message sent from the angels, but the angels frequently like to use song to get their messages across to us.

Audible whispers

Speaking directly with us as though it was a conversation between a human and human can be a very challenging task for both the angels and the person they are helping. You are most likely to come across this method of communication while you are drifting of to sleep or coming out of a deep sleep, as the brain is more relaxed and you are more susceptible to hearing them. It may be just your name being said, or a word that will have meaning to you. While these audible whispers are quick and not long sentences, they can be an experience that you will remember for a long time and affirm to yourself that the angels are around you and looking out for you.

Over hearing conversations

Another way that the angels may communicate with you is by the very subtle way of making your ears pick up a nearby conversation. It may be a situation where you are sat day dreaming on a bus ride home for a day at college or work and you over hear someone having a conversation on a mobile phone giving advice to their friend. That same advice may be of use to you and something you have been asking the angels about.

As sounds are usually a quick sign from the angels, it can be very easy to miss. Make sure you are open to the angels and ask them to help you to hear their messages loud and clear.

Don't be alarmed if you don't hear the angels, these types of messages are hard to get and you may find that your spiritual communication strengths lay with one of the many other methods that the angels communicate to you with.

You may also experience any of the above methods of communication when you least expect it. Such as with other methods of communicating with the angels, it's not something that can be forced, and everybody's experience will be very different and unique.

Chapter Activity: This chapter activity is something to do in your everyday life rather than just during meditation. Try to notice all the sounds going on around you. Bring your attention to the sound of the car driving past, the sound of the birds singing in the trees or even the sound of the boiler turning on.

The more you start to become aware of the sounds around you including background noise, then the chances of you hearing the angels communicating with you are going to be much higher.

SEEING THE ANGELS

Some people can see the angels, either as orbs of light, (which is covered in the chapter 'signs you may receive from the angels').

Not everyone will see the angels with their own eyes, and not everyone will see angels in the same way.

A popular way that the angels may appear to people is in the form of orbs of light. Usually witnessed in the corner of your eye-line.

These orbs may appear tiny and will disappear as quickly as they appeared.

In any of the forms that we have mentioned, you will usually see angels with a white aura or light. If you are connecting with the archangels then you may see the aura as a particular colour that relates to the archangel. See the chapter activity for more information on this.

Angels can appear in many different sizes. Archangels tend to appear bigger due to their more powerful energy.

Chapter Activity: This activity involves familiarising yourself with each of the archangels colours. This is so if you see a coloured orb, then you will find it easier and quicker to know which archangel is showing you their presence. Use the sheet on the next page as a cheat sheet to help you learn.

"You cannot be lonely if you like the person
you're alone with."

- Dr. Wayne Dyer

Archangel	Colour
Archangel Ariel	Light Pink
Archangel Azrael	Cream White
Archangel Chamuel	Pale Green
Archangel Gabriel	Orange
Archangel Haniel	Baby Blue
Archangel Jeremiel	Dark Purple
Archangel Jophiel	Red
Archangel Metatron	Violet
Archangel Michael	Vivid Blue/ Purple
Archangel Raguel	Baby Blue
Archangel Raphael	Vivid Green
Archangel Raziel	Rainbow
Archangel Sandalphon	Turquoise
Archangel Uriel	Yellow
Archangel Zadkiel	Indigo

HOW TO FEEL THE ANGELS

Feeling the angels touch can be quite a rare form of communication. This is usually because it doesn't give any clear answers to your questions or requests. Feeling the brush of an angel is usually felt when in deep mediation, or just as you are about to fall asleep.

The angels tend to communicate this way just to let you know they are present, around you, and comforting you.

Feeling the angels can vary from the brush of something against your skin, tingles across your body, most often the back of the head and neck, and also a pleasant breeze across you even though there's no other possible source.

If you do feel a spirits presence with some of the above signs then do not be alarmed. You may be first surprised, but you will soon feel the love of the angels around you.

Another way you may feel the angels is in an emotional sense. You may feel an overwhelming sense of joy. This is a sign from the angels that they are right by your side, protecting you and sharing their love with you. This overwhelming energy you feel can be enough to bring tears of happiness to your eyes. You may not get this sensation all the time that you connect or meditate with the angels but it is certainly a spectacular and magical feeling and one you should let them know that you are open to.

Chapter Activity: For this chapter activity, it involves a meditation. First find a comfortable place and position, you could even play some non lyrical music in the background.

Once you have found yourself in a meditative state. Imagine an angel positioned behind you, now visualise there wings are big and beautiful, they then envelope you with their wings. You feel so much joy and peace and so so safe. Just use this meditation to bask in this amazing energy. When you feel ready to end the meditation, thank the angel for their presence, and start to come out of your meditation slowly.

USING ANGEL CARDS

Angel cards are an amazing way to connect to the angels. They are easy to use, give accurate readings and they allow you to get clear responses back from the angels.

Tarot cards can be used in place of angel cards or oracle cards. Some people may prefer to use angel cards if they have been put off from using tarot in the past. This darker reputation isn't helped by mainstream media as well as the infamous 'death' card. (FYI, it does not mean that you are going to suddenly die if you ever pull the death card).

Use whichever you feel most comfortable with and guided to.

There are a number of decks out there, the most popular ones are by publisher Hay House, who created the decks with the author Doreen Virtue. However there are many different authors and angel card makers out there, or you could even try making your own.

Here are some basic steps to get started!

Step 1 - Bless the deck and protect yourself

This step will remove any residual energy left in your card deck from previous readings. It will give your future readings a fresh start. There a few methods you can do such as smudging your cards with sage or visualising white light round your cards. A common method that is often recommended is to take the card deck in your non dominant hand and with your dominant hand knock your hand on the deck as though you're knocking on a door. This will *bang* the energy out of the cards.

Step 2 - Shuffle your deck

Shuffling the cards in your deck is as simple as it sounds. You can shuffle like a Vegas pro or you can place each card out on the floor/table and then pick them all back up in a random order, whichever way you pick, you can't go wrong.

Step 3 - Picking the cards

There are a few different ways that you can do this, just trust your gut instincts as to which you feel you prefer.

One method is, once you have stopped shuffling the cards, just pick the cards from the top. You may also prefer to shuffle and then stop when you feel guided to do, take the card and then shuffle and repeat until you have the number of cards required for your reading.

When you are shuffling the cards you may see a card that just *pops* out from the deck. This is the angels letting you know to include this card in your reading. If this happens after you have picked up the required number of cards for your reading, still include this card that has popped out in your reading.

When you place the cards down, make sure they are facing downwards, this is so you don't get distracted and can interpret each card separately.

Step 4 - Interpreting the cards

Interpreting the cards is more about trusting your intuition and gut instinct rather than using the guide book that comes with the card deck. Important things to look out for are where do your eyes look toward on the card first, do your feelings suddenly change when you turn over the card, do you start to picture anything in your head or start to smell a good or bad fragrance. All these signals will help you to summarise what the angels want to tell you about the card that has been picked.

If your card has text, this can help you to make sense of a card and you should include them in your reading as text is just as descriptive as seeing an image.

Using card layouts are a popular way to structure a reading, for example a 3 card lay out. The first would be for the past situation, the second is for the present situation and the third card would be what will happen in the future.

These lay outs can be as complex or as simple as you wish them to be, you may even feel you only want to pick one card, this is fine. There is no set of rules as you are following the divine guidance of your intuition.

Step 5 - Finishing the reading

Once you feel the reading has finished, thank the spirits and angels involved. If you still feel a bit dizzy and ungrounded, do a simple grounding exercise such as visualising roots growing from your feet all the way deep in to the Earth. You may also like to hold a grounding crystal such as tourmaline.

You may decide to meditate and reflect on the reading you have just done in which you may receive further guidance.

Working with angel cards or any oracle cards is a magical way to connect to spirit and to receive clear messages. You may find that you often pick out the same card when working with a deck.

Once you have finished with your card deck you may like to keep them in the box that they came in from the manufacturer as this will keep them dry and safe. However, if you feel guided, why not try a beautiful wooden box that you can buy from an holistic shop, or you may even like to keep them on an altar and wrapped in silk.

Chapter Activity: In this chapter activity I want you to give yourself or a friend a reading. You may want to do one that uses just 3 cards for a while so you can build your confidence. As you get more practice with your cards, your readings will improve and give you or your recipient clearer readings.

"Love is the only force capable of transforming
an enemy into a friend."

- Martin Luther King, Jr

ANGEL CRYSTALS

Buying and working with crystals tends to be one of main ways people are introduced into spirituality. Crystals are beautiful gifts from mother earth which are imbued with natures power. Each crystal has its own unique properties. Some crystals are especially useful to work with when connecting to and attracting the angels. The crystals listed below may be useful for you in this journey.

Rose quartz:

This beautiful pink stone is also known as the love stone and tends to be associated with the heart chakra. This crystal is handy to have by during work as it helps to reduce stress and enhances feelings of love.

Angelite:

This is another crystal that can help attract more love in to your life. It's calming and soothing properties make it particularly useful when you're getting ready to meditate or connect to the angels.

Angel aura quartz:

This is the perfect crystal to help you make positive changes in your life especially if you are on a new path. An example would be doing this course to increase your connection to the angels, this is a useful crystal to have around. It's also a great crystal to use when cleansing your aura.

Azeztulite:

While not a common crystal this will bring good energy to any space that the crystal is in. It is a member of the quartz family however some people are said to find it's strong vibrations difficult to deal with at first and that it takes daily exercise and time with the crystal to help you adapt.

Amethyst:

A very popular crystal that has been used for centuries. In modern spiritual times the amethyst crystal brings healing and calmness. This crystal is great at strengthening your intuition and helping you to trust your gut instincts. If you find yourself getting stressed and you want to communicate with the angels, have a bit of time with an amethyst stone to help calm you down. Your messages will then be heard louder and clearer by the angels.

Celestite:

This crystal is often known as the angels crystal. It has been associated with the divine and celestial sky (heaven) for years throughout history as some civilisations even believed it was a piece of fallen sky. Both magical and mystical this crystal is uplifting, improves your self confidence and raises your spiritual vibration that is perfect for connecting to the angelic realms.

Emerald:

This vivid green crystal is usually associated with the heart chakra and is sometimes called the stone of successful love. Have an emerald crystal near you if you wish to learn about the future, or if you're doing a reading that focuses on the year ahead. It also helps you to stay focused on an important study task and is a great protection stone.

Seraphinite:

Named after the seraphim, the highest order of angels, this is a high vibrational and energetic stone. Use this crystal to energise your aura. Particularly useful when preparing to give a reading or while you meditate.

Moldavite:

This is another high vibrational crystal and is great to have when you communicate with the angels as it acts as a superb psychic protector. It is believed that negative and low vibrational spirits find it hard to connect to your aura when moldavite is present. Some people may find it's energy too intense when they start working with moldavite so practice with it just a little bit at a time until you gradually adapt to its powerful energy.

Chapter Activity: Find a crystal from the above list. Firstly, make sure your crystal is cleansed. An easy way to do this is to leave it in moon light over night.

You will now do a quick prayer on the crystal. Hold it in your hands and recite:

Dear Universe, please bless this crystal, may its powers be strengthened, and used as a beacon to show the angels in to my dreams, to give me healing, guidance and love. Thank you.

Now place the crystal under your pillow. As you go to sleep each night, the blessed crystal with aid the angels coming in to your dreams to give you guidance and messages.

"Create a life that feels good on the inside, not just one that looks good on the outside."

- Unknown

GOING WITH THE FLOW IN LIFE

Communicating with the angels and asking them for help is all about having faith in the angels and the universe.

Once you have asked them for help, trust that the angels are helping you in the best possible way. Don't force a certain path in your head. The angels can guide us to greater things than we first may have imagined.

Trusting in life is a whole new way of living. It allows you to stop worrying about things you can't control, releasing fear and appreciating all that is good in your life, no matter how small it may appear to be.

Even if bad things may happen to us in our life, knowing you have the full support of the angels and archangels is a comforting piece of knowledge to have.

Finding our way in this lifetime can be a challenge but by involving the angels and allowing them to help us you can be guided in the best direction for you.

As you become more trustworthy of the universe and letting the angels work their magic then you will find that the messages and signs that you receive are *clearer* and *louder* than ever as you are reducing the chance of blocking any help coming your way.

Chapter Activity: Write down a list of 10 things that you are grateful for. e.g. I am thankful that I can see the world around me. I am grateful that I have plenty of food in my cupboards. Why not try this task every day for a week and you will soon see that you have a lot of to be grateful for.

GROUNDING

When connecting to the angels and spiritual realms you may find yourself starting to go a bit *spacey*, similar to the expression when someone says 'you're away with the fairies'.

Remember that we are on Earth with a purpose so try not to spend all your time disconnected.

There are a number of ways that you can ground yourself. Let's take a look...

Crystals

Certain crystals have grounding properties. All you need to do is hold the crystal and let its special abilities ground you back to the Earth's energies. The following crystals can be used for grounding; petrified wood, tourmaline (black), obsidian (black).

Visualisation

This one is popular as the visualisation can be carried on and blend in with your meditation. Visualising that roots are growing downwards from your body (so out through the bottom of your feet), and imagine the roots are growing all the way down through the earth as though they are *rooting* you to Earth.

Having a glass of water

This one is as simple as it sounds. Having a glass of water can help ground your energies back to Earth.

Going in nature

This method of grounding is essentially just going outside, if you're feeling particularly detached then try go to your nearest woodland or nature park. Your garden or local park is a great way to ground yourself. If you are able to, try to take shoes and socks of so that your bare feet touch the Earth. You will soon feel its grounding properties as you *come back down to Earth.*

You can use any of these methods at any time to ground yourself. No method is better than another, it is all down to personal preference. It may be that at a particular moment you are only able to visualise grounding since there are other people around you, or you may find that since you're meditating in your garden on a sunny day that the *going in nature* method is your preferred choice.

If you discover another method that you prefer, use it. Even if it is not written down in this guide or in another resource, if it works for you and you're following your internal guidance then there is no wrong method to ground yourself.

Chapter Activity: This chapter activity involves a grounding visualisation. You can use this exactly or adapt it to your own personal preference.

Imagine yourself standing in a beautiful meadow with wild flowers, blue sky and the sun shining brightly. Nearby is a waterfall. You are standing tall and proud and then you start to visualise great tree roots coming from your feet. See them in your mind pushing through the earth beneath you.

As they go deeper within the earth they pass large piece of powerful quartz crystals, imagine the roots tangling round these large and beautiful crystals hidden deep within the earths core.

Once you feel grounded and guided to stop by your feelings and intuition just imagine the roots fading and take a deep breath.

You may decide to take just parts of this visualisation exercise or you may decide to do it while standing on the lawn in your garden with your eyes wide open. Follow your intuition and you won't go wrong.

"Live as if you were to die tomorrow. Learn as if you were to live forever."

- Mahatma Gandhi

The End.